MOVE AND GET HEALTHY!

GET MOVING WITH FRIENDS AND FAMILY

WRITTEN BY
NADIA HIGGINS

ILLUSTRATED BY
TATEVIK AVAKYAN

Content Consultant:
Jonathan Martin
Physical Education Teacher, Nova Classical Academy

magic wagon

VISIT US AT WWW.ABDOPUBLISHING.COM

Published by Magic Wagon, a division of the ABDO Group, PO Box 398166, Minneapolis, MN 55439. Copyright © 2012 by Abdo Consulting Group, Inc.

Looking Glass Library™ is a trademark and logo of Magic Wagon.

Printed in the United States of America, North Mankato, Minnesota.
102011
012012

Text by Nadia Higgins
Illustrations by Tatevik Avakyan
Edited by Melissa York
Design and production by Emily Love

Library of Congress Cataloging-in-Publication Data

Higgins, Nadia.
Get moving with friends and family / by Nadia Higgins ; illustrated by Tatevik Avakyan.
    p. cm. — (Move and get healthy!)
Includes index.
ISBN 978-1-61641-860-1
1. Physical fitness for children—Juvenile literature. I. Avakyan, Tatevik, 1983- iill. II. Title.
GV443.H46 2012
613.7083—dc23
                                                            2011033082

TABLE OF CONTENTS

60 MINUTES EVERY DAY

Playing sports and other games are great ways to get moving. But exercise can be simple, too. It can be gardening with your mom. Or it can be walking to the bus stop with your friends. Any moving that gets your heart pumping is exercise!

Your body needs 60 minutes of moving every day. It doesn't have to be all at once. Here's an example from one kid's day:

Climbing monkey bars at recess: 10 minutes

Playing tag at recess: 15 minutes

Riding bike after school: 20 minutes

Raking leaves: 15 minutes

10 + 15 + 20 + 15 = 60

Moving keeps you fit and trim. It makes your hear-, muscles, and bones strong. Moving makes you feel good. It can help you sleep at night and do better in school, too.

The best kinds of moving are with friends and family. Good company turns exercising into playing. Dance with a friend. Play tag with your sister. Then those 60 minutes go by in a second!

SAFETY FIRST . . .

Don't forget these tips to keep you safe:

❋ Drink lots of water, especially on hot days.

❋ Wear socks and sneakers. You might trip on flip-flops.

❋ Look out for cars if you are near the street.

❋ How far away from your house are you allowed to go? How often do you need to check in? Ask your grown-ups about the rules.

❋ Strap on a helmet before you grab your bike or scooter.

❋ Taking a swim? An adult needs to be watching at all times.

❋ Don't overdo it. Sweaty and tired? Good. Sick, can't breathe, or hurt? Stop and get help.

GET SWEATY

Ride your bike up a hill. Or, paint a fence with your dad. Pretty soon, you're hot and sweaty. You are using energy. That makes heat. Your body is doing its job of cooling you down.

Sweat cools your body like a sprinkler. Glands inside your skin make sweat. The sweat comes out through tiny holes, or pores. You have thousands of pores all over your body.

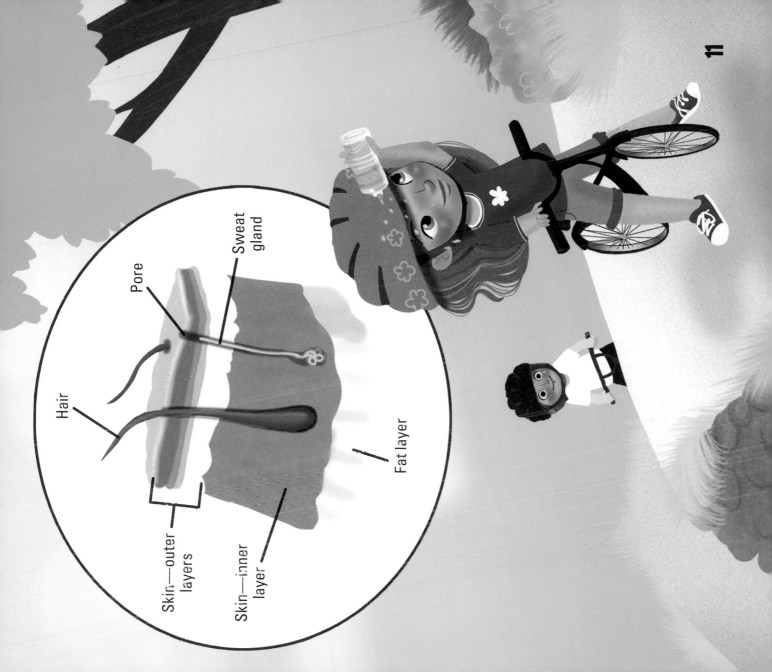

Hair

Pore

Sweat gland

Skin—outer layers

Skin—inner layer

Fat layer

Sweating means you are getting plenty of exercise. Check out these fun games. They are sure to make you sweat!

TEAM TAG

Play tag in teams. One team is the taggers. The other is the runners. Mark off an area. That's the "jail." When a runner gets tagged, she has to go to jail. She gets free when another runner tags her.

ATTACK OF THE BLOB!

One person starts as It, and she tags another kid. They hold hands and chase together until they tag another kid. Now that third kids joins their chain. The "blob" of kids keeps chasing and tagging. The game ends when everyone is It.

13

STRONG HEART

You jump rope to the end of the block. You and your friend practice a dance. Your heart is beating faster. You take shorter breaths. That means you are getting aerobic exercise. This type of exercise makes your heart stronger.

Your heart is about the size of your fist. It beats between 70 and 120 times per minute. Your heart can pump twice that fast when you are playing hard.

HERE ARE SOME GREAT WAYS
TO WORK YOUR HEART:

swimming

running

riding your bike

skating

dancing

walking fast

HOW DOES THE HEART WORK?

Your muscles need oxygen to work. You breathe in oxygen from the air. The oxygen goes into your blood. Your heart pumps. It sends blood all around your body. The blood travels inside long, thin tubes called vessels.

When you play hard, you breathe faster. You take in more oxygen. Your heart beats faster. It sends more oxygen to your muscles.

Check out more fun ways to get your heart pumping:

500

One kid is the thrower. Everyone else stands in a group nearby. The thrower turns his back to the other kids. Then he throws the ball toward them. He yells a number between 50 and 500. The ball catcher earns that number of points. The first kid to get 500 points becomes the next thrower.

RIGHT, LEFT, OR STRAIGHT?

Walk out your door with a grown-up. Will you turn right, left, or go straight? You choose! Keep going until you come to another street. Choose another direction, and another. Keep going for 15 minutes. Then turn around. Try to lead your grown-up back home.

STRONG MUSCLES

Pushing, pulling, and lifting is called strength training. Strength training happens in short, powerful bursts. It makes your muscles stronger.

Bodybuilders lift weights to build their muscles. But you can push, pull, and lift your own body. Race your friends across the monkey bars. Build a snowman with your dad. Or, pull a friend in a wagon.

HERE ARE SOME GREAT WAYS TO WORK YOUR MUSCLES:

push-ups	tug-of-war	monkey bars
pull-ups	climbing	squat jumps
swimming	rowing	lunges

Swimming is one of the best forms of strength training. Try this fun game with family and friends:

SHIPS ACROSS THE OCEAN

The player who is It stands in the middle of the pool and closes her eyes. All the other players line up on one end. Then, It yells, "Ships across the ocean!" All the other players have to swim to the other end. It tries to tag them. Tagged kids become It, too. The game ends when everybody's been tagged.

If you do not have a pool, you can run through a sprinkler, set up a Slip 'N Slide, or have a squirt gun fight.

STRETCH!

Stretch your arms up, up, up into the sky. It feels so good! Stretching makes you flexible, too. That makes you a star in yoga, gymnastics, and ballet. It also protects your muscles from getting hurt.

Sit on the floor with your legs out in front of you. Is it easy to touch your toes? That means you have good flexibility.

HERE ARE SOME GREAT WAYS TO WORK ON FLEXIBILITY:

yoga

dance

stretching

gymnastics

martial arts

HEALTHY HABITS

Turning off the TV and going outside are healthy habits. Just turning off the TV will make you move more. Step outside to fly a kite or bike to a friend's house.

Adding healthy habits to your life takes a lot of practice. It could take two months before you are used to watching less TV. But healthy habits add up. They help keep you fit. And they're fun!

COMMERCIAL CONTEST

If you are watching a TV show, have a contest with your friends or family. See who can do the most jumping jacks during the commercial breaks.

Here are a couple of ways to start healthy habits:

USE THOSE LEGS!

Tell a grown-up to choose the farthest spot in a parking lot. Or, get off a few stops early on the bus or subway. Walk or bike to get to school or to the store.

COUNT YOUR STEPS

Kids should try to take about 12,000 steps every day. You can buy a pedometer to count your steps and wear it all day. Or, count your steps for 10 minutes. Then, if you walk for half an hour, multiply your number of steps by three. If you walk for an hour, multiply by six.

What other little things can you do to move more each day? What will you do tomorrow? Who will you invite to move with you?

KEEP MOVING

1. A park near you needs your help with weeding, picking up garbage, building trails, and more. Invite your friends to pitch in this coming National Public Lands Day on September 24. Join thousands of volunteers across the country by cleaning up a favorite outdoor spot. To find a site or to register your group, visit NPLD's Web site at www.publiclandsday.org.

2. The president is challenging you to move! Earn the President's Active Lifestyle Award by staying active and tracking your progress. Do 60 minutes of activity five days a week for six out of eight weeks. Even better, do it with a friend. Sign up at the PALA Web site: http://www.presidentschallenge.org/challenge/active/index.shtml.

3. Do you have a favorite cousin or another relative who lives far away? Set up a time to talk weekly. Ask a grown-up if you can use a cell phone and walk while you catch up.

4. Make a recess club at school. Every day at recess, play one of the games from this book. (And think of a cool name for your club, too!) Use your imagination to make up your own games.

5. Instead of going to the movies, go bowling, mini-golfing, or hiking. Another idea is to walk to the movie theater. Or, drive part of the way there and walk the rest.

WORDS TO KNOW

aerobic exercise—exercise, such as running and jumping, that makes your heart stronger.

energy—being able to do things without feeling tired.

flexible—being able to bend or stretch far without feeling pain.

habit—an action or small activity that you are used to doing often.

muscle—body tissue, or layers of cells, that help the body move.

oxygen—a colorless gas that humans and animals need to breathe.

pedometer—a digital tool that counts the number of steps taken. A pedometer looks like a digital watch and clips to a belt or waistband.

yoga—a kind of exercise that involves deep breathing and holding your body in special positions, or poses.

LEARN MORE

BOOKS

Gogerly, Liz. *Exercise*. New York, NY: Crabtree, 2009.

Hewitt, Sally, and Angela Royston. *My Body*. Buffalo, NY: Firefly Books, 2009.

Rockwell, Lizzy. *The Busy Body Book: A Kid's Guide to Fitness*. New York, NY: Dragonfly Books, 2008.

Spinelli, Eileen. *Miss Fox's Class Shapes Up*. Chicago, IL: Albert Whitman & Co., 2011.

WEB SITES

To learn more about being active with friends and family, visit ABDO Group online at **www.abdopublishing.com**. Web sites about being active with friends and family are featured on our Book Links page. These links are routinely monitored and updated to provide the most current information available.

INDEX